Book of Twisted Tales and Rhymes

By

Ruth Doyle

ISBN: 978-1-914130-74-8

This book is in honour of my
late husband Paul Doyle.

OTHER TITLES BY IMPSPIRED

Learning to Climb the Mountain –
by Ann Christine Tabaka

Periodic Stories V3 -
by Jim Bates

Out of the Chrysalis –
by Mary Farrell

Rattlesnakes and Flattops
by Mackenzie Thorn

Lily –
by Karl Diaz

Irish Hares & Seahorses –
by North Coast Writers

Classical Adaptations –
by Susie Gharib

Contents

Introduction

Delve into my magical world of
Twisted fairy tales and rhymes
And go to a place that you haven't been
Before.

Amazonia (story)

Once upon a time there was a kingdom ruled by a wicked queen Granita. This wasn't actually her real name, but her subjects called her this because in the Amazonian language it means heart of stone.
She was a lazy queen - couldn't even be bothered to write her own speeches. So, she got her courtiers to write them for her.
Unfortunately for them she was never happy with what they wrote, and either executed them or sent them to Ebania to get exiled.
Well, she had banished so many subjects, that she had to go through the kingdom looking for replacements.
After many, many years she found three people who said they were used to writing speeches.
So, she put them to work.
Little was she aware that they were not just any kind of people they were magical and their relatives were some of the people that had been exiled.
Well, actually two were magical the third was the witch from hell who cast a spell to get rid of Granita
and bring back the true ruler the Princess of Ebania.
They all lived happily ever after in peace and harmony.

The end.

Astro Day (Poem)

Today in Astro land it is a special day,
where all the fairies from near or far,
they come to play a game
that is based upon a star.

Each time they must be first,
to see how many stars they can burst.
And the team that has burst more,
they get the keys to the fairy-castle door.
Where they will meet the fairy queen,
who is sitting so serene.
They also get some dinner,
for they are, of course, a winner.

Bluebell the Fairy

Come down into the wood today,
where bluebell the fairy does dwell,
You will find her most of the time,
sitting on her shell.

She sits down as pretty as can be,
as she is the bluebell fairy.
If ever you are in trouble
and don't know what to do,
always ask for bluebell
and she will look after you.

She is there on every hour,
protecting every petal in every flower.
And when the day has gone she will fly,
to her little home in the sky.

The Boy

There once lived a boy
who was so very bright,
he could change the
day into night.
Cos he lived
in magic land he
made it all himself,
and cos he was
so clever he got
lots of wealth.
But still this boy
was full of woe,
cos back to home
he wanted to go.
Then he made up
a magic spell,
now he is happy
and very well.
Now he is back at
home for a while,
and on his face
there is a smile.

Castana and the Ball (story)

In fairyland it was that time
of the year for the ball.
But unfortunately for Castana she may not
be able to attend again.
As to go to the ball you have to have a
special talent.
All the other fairies had a talent whether
it was to sing or dance and lots of other
gifts.
So poor Castana sat on the shore and was
so unhappy she just cried.
Then all of a sudden there was a big flash
and the fairy godmother appeared.
She was holding a jar and lo and behold
her tears inside the jar had
turned into silver stars.
Castana couldn't believe it, so now she
was allowed to go to the ball.
And the stars came out of the jar,
and flew around the room and
everyone was amazed.

Castle

This is the castle
where fairies go,
once a year
to see a show.
People come for
miles around
just so they
can hear
the sound.
The melodies
are so unreal
they are there
to make the
fairies feel
so very, very good.
As they walk back
thru the magic wood,
they will not
shed a tear,
cos they know they'll
be coming back
next year.

Christmas Disaster

There's trouble brewing in the north pole,
everything is out of control.
They have run out of fairy dust,
and getting some more is a must.
Before Christmas time is here,
all the elves are full of fear.

There is no way to make a toy,
for every girl and every boy.
Santa Claus doesn't know how
to carry on,
now all the fairy dust is gone.

Then along came Donner and Blitzen
with the help of Cupid and Vixen.
They had enough to get to fairyland
and they can get some more,
the place they have to get it, is Santa's Surplus Store.

So now children - do not worry,
for Christmas will be back in a hurry.
Everything will now be on track,
once the reindeers do get back.

Christmas

On Christmas eve, you will not see
children gathering around the tree.
for it has now been said,
children are tucked up safe in bed.

Cos it is a magic time,
when Santa Claus is around,
in the morning, when they wake up
lovely presents will be found.

So, all you children go off to bed
after you have said your prayers,
and in the morning, when you wake up
you can all go downstairs.

Cinderella Time Warp

Once upon a time there was a girl called Cinder.
Her sisters sent her out, for to get some tinder.
So, she went out and saw a sign,
said we have tinder it's all online.

Well, she thought, this will be no good,
it doesn't look like any wood.
So, she thought she would take a chance
a young man appeared, like she was in a trance.

He sent her a message. This is what it said:
"My lovely Cinder I think we should wed."

Disneyland

Welcome to Disneyland
where everything is so very grand.
You can go into a house,
just to see Minnie Mouse.
If you have any luck,
you can also see Donald Duck.
Then maybe you would like to go,
there to see Pinocchio.
And before the day turns into night,
don't forget to see Snow White.

Elemental Fairy

I am the fairy
of the earth,
I will sprinkle fairy
dust for all I'm worth.
I am the fairy
of the fire,
I like to keep
people warm before
I retire.
I am the fairy
of the breeze,
my wish is
for all to please.
I am the fairy
of the air,
I like to show
everyone that
I do care.
So, if you see
my elemental,
my role in life
is to be so gentle.

Fairy Medley

Red riding hood went out for the day
but alas she got lost.
Then she saw a figure, turned out to be
Old Jack Frost.

She wondered down into the wood
where she spied Robin hood.
But the problem is you see,
he was looking for Friar Tuck
and on the tree he got stuck.

Then along came William Tell,
and he happened to have a cell.
So, he rang to get the crew,
and they knew just what to do.
Not only did they get Robin Hood off the tree,
but got Red Riding Hood back home for tea.

Fairytale Book

I have just found an ideal book,
for anyone to take a look.
Well for children, it is very grand,
tis' a passport to fairyland.

When you think of a fairy-tale,
then you get transported there,
but only for a while.
You can be Red Riding Hood
or even Snow White,
And also, Cinderella
before she went out for the night.

But alas with this book, you can only see,
if you are as old as seven or as young as three.
You can be Rapunzel inside the tower,
but only stay there for an hour.
And only once a year - or this book will disappear.

Flower Fairy

Here am I as pretty
as can be,
people call me
The Flower Fairy.
I have been invited
it is so very grand,
it's at the palace
and is in fairyland.
It's a special day
I'm going there
for tea,
There will be cake
and ice cream
especially for me.
And after I
have finished
and go home instead,
then I will rest
upon my fairy bed.

Georgy Porgy

Georgy Porgy pudding
and pie,
he ate so much it
made him cry
So, he decided to riot,
and put himself
back on his diet.
And now he eats
his greens and fruit,
he can now walk around
in his suit.
For he feels so very well,
he is so happy he can
ring his bell.

Hansel and Gretel

Revisited

One day Hansel and Gretel went into the city,
and loved it cos it looked so pretty.
Not like so long ago - nearly went into the fire,
this is a modern world, and they were dressed
in perfect attire.

They had heard of candy land
it was a big store,
with chocolate and sweets galore.
You can have lots to eat,
but alas there is a trick to this treat.

You must stay, where you are told,
for when the candies are all sold,
everything will be out of hand
and there will be no more candy land!

Hickory Dickory Dock

Hickory dickory dock,
Here am I, stuck inside this clock,
There is no way that I can get out
Even though I scream and shout.
Maybe someone will hear me soon,
It could be from another room?
Until then, I will stay
Maybe help will come my way.

Iced Match

One day the ice fairy she did go,
it was for a walk in the snow.
On her way she paid the cost,
to the Toll man called Jack Frost.
Then to her surprise, there in front of her eyes
Stood a snowman near the wood,
on a pedestal whence he stood.
She had never seen one before,
and this one she did adore.
So, a spell she did cast,
that the love they had would really last.
So now they are together,
with a love that would last forever.

Jack and the Beanstalk

Well jack went out one day for a walk,
his magic beans grew from a stalk.
They did turn into a tree,
so, he climbed up to have a see.

Inside the tree there was a door
just past a little twig,
and just inside he saw a giant who was very big.
The giant said sit down with me,
We can have some cake and tea.
Well Jack came in, he was surprised,
in fact, could not believe his eyes.
For the giant was gentle you see,
and said to him thanks for the tea.

The giant said: "if one day you're passing by…"
"…come again and have some pie."
Jack said he would try his best,
but now was going home to rest.

Keys of Magic

There is a story, I have heard tell,
it was told by Tinkerbell.
You must go through the enchanted wood
to the magic tree,
there within the branches lies the magic key.

You can get the keys to the kingdom,
if you say a special rhyme,
Then you will be granted a visit
for a very short time.

But you must be wary
For somewhere lies one called the Black Fairy
she will take you, out of the wood,
so don't go near, it won't be good.
Go and find magic, it's your pleasure,
and have memories, that you can treasure.

The King

One day in the fairy kingdom there lived a king,
problem was he couldn't remember anything.
Cos' he had been cursed by one so dark,
when he was walking in the park.
He asked for help and it did come,
from the fairy called Magic Mum.
She made a magic spell, now the king can remember
well.

The Land of Blue (story)

Once upon a time there was a magical place
called the Land of Blue,
till the evil witch Esmeralda came
and declared herself queen.
Ever since then the fairies were not happy.
The evil witch had banned fairy magic.
Because of this the trees and flowers were dying.
The animals had all left for a happier land.
Now the Blue Land was a very lonely and
dark place.
One day a fairy who was very brave
managed to escape because she wanted
to find her godfather who happened to
be a wizard.
Well, once they met up again, he came
back with her with his wizard's book
and cast a spell while the evil witch was asleep.
And lo and behold she disappeared in a
big puff of smoke.
And something wonderful happened
the Snow Queen did appear, all the
animals came back and the flowers and
trees were growing once more,
and happiness came back to the land.

The end.

The Boy and the Leprechaun (story)

My name is Seamus and I come from a very poor village called Dun Fore.
Well, you can probably tell by the title that we are very poor.
Every year when one of our lads reaches the age of twelve he must go on a quest.
What we do have is very fine leather that has been sewn by the villagers.
The purpose of this quest is to find a leprechaun, who if the legend is true will lead us to the pot of gold at the end of the rainbow.
Well, I travelled for many days and found a little shoemakers shop right on the edge of the forest.
Inside was one of the little people who was very wary of humans and didn't want to know.
Then I told him I was in possession of the most-finest leather if we made a deal it was all his.
Well to my surprise the deal was struck.
Then all of a sudden, I could hear music and lo and behold there were leprechauns everywhere dancing a jig.
Then I was told they too had a legend that a poor boy called Seamus would offer them leather and this would lead them to the pot of gold at the end of the rainbow.
And just like magic we found it and not only did we share it but they all came back to my village and we all lived happy after.
The end.

Life and Times of Humpty Dumpty

Once I was an egg but felt so wrong,
For life in a shell, I didn't belong.
Fed up of sitting on this wall,
By doing this am bound to fall.
Made up my mind the time was right,
I will take part in magic tonight.
The wizard he came to me,
He gave me one wish for free.
It made me feel so much joy,
Now I've turned into a boy.
I find my life is now complete,
I have fingers and also feet.
Now I can have so much glee,
And will be the perfect me.

Lion, Witch and Wardrobe

There once was a witch
She was scared as can be,
When she saw a lion
Behind a tree.
She was walking
In the wood one day,
When a lion came
Looking for some prey.
Her name was Esmeralda
She was full of shame,
And didn't think a lion
Would find her easy game.
She espied a cottage
And walked through the door,
Inside there was a wardrobe
Just sitting on the floor.
Esmeralda went inside
And thought it was a
Great place to hide.
But this was a magic wardrobe
And it took her far away,
To a wonderful place where
Good witches go and stay.
Now she is happy as can be,
All her friends invite her
Around their place for tea.

Lonesome Witch

Once upon a time
there lived a witch
her name was
Gertrude Laval,
If she had anything
to do she would
make people so unwell.
Now she is a lonesome crone,
her magic is no longer there
she just sits all alone,
with no one who
would care.
For karma came one day
it was to her door,
and evil that she had
she has got no more.
So if you're ever
down the wood
do not be afraid,
for whatever she
has done before
justice has now
been paid.

Lost Fairy

Lost within the fairy kingdom
I am just another fae,
Wondered so far from home
Think this fairy has lost her way.
For I went out with fairy kin
Strayed within the wood,
Will I get home soon?
Or maybe lost for good.
But think now things are looking bright,
Ahead I see a fairy light.
Now here stands tall
A happy fae,
I truly have found my
Way home today.

Incy Wincy Spider

Incy wincy spider was as
Happy as can be,
Until she got stuck
On top of a tree.
Then along came Boris
He was her friend,
And told Incy this
Is not the end.
He then managed
To help her down,
And they lived happy ever after
In Arachnia which is spider town.

Magic Door

In the magic castle
There is a door,
Enter and see
What you haven't before.
On display there is a star,
Its on a shelf in a jar.
In this story seldom told,
Enter and see the pot of gold.
There's lots more for you to see,
Leprechaun's wizards and
A lovely fairy.
So please join me through this door,
Where you will find magic galore.

Magic Tree

Here is the magic tree
where animals
find a home,
it is always there
where ever
they may roam.
First of all you
have the deer
who will find lots
of comfort here.
Then for the badgers
rabbits and hare,
there is nothing
to compare.
So, animals of
the world if
you're feeling tragic,
come down to
the special tree
where you will
find some magic.

Magic Trip

One day I was sitting at home
with my brother Jamie we
were both so bored.
There was nothing much for us to do.
Then all of a sudden the window blew
open and a letter blew inside.
This was so strange well we opened it
It was addressed to us Lily and Jamie.
We found we had won a one off
ticket to go for the day to a magic castle.
Before we had time to think a rainbow
cloud appeared outside and we were
floating through the air.
And lo and behold we were at the castle
having a guided tour, then having a
banquet as we were prince and princess
for the day.
Then after a dance round the ballroom.
All of a sudden, we were home again.
What a wonderful magical day we had
with lovely memories.

Magic Horse

Welcome to Fairyland
where everything
is o' so grand
now today we
have a clip
it's all about
this magic trip
you can go
all round
the course
with Fiona
our magic horse
loaned out
for us today
from princess
Aerofay.

Mary and the Sheep

Mary had a little lamb
she also had some sheep,
people were always knocking
on her door because they
Couldn't get to sleep.
She sent them
round the corner,
to a boy called
Little Jack Horner.
Who had a
special trick,
so, you could
get to sleep quick.
Well, I don't know
how this came about,
or what he told
people to do,
all I know past
Mary's house there
Isn't any queue.

Mary had a Little Lamb

Mary had a little lamb,
she also had a dog,
she took them out
and they got lost
inside the fog.
The dog was quite unusual
as he had the power to talk,
He said to Mary why did
you take us for this walk.
Mary said to the dog
when I take you out again,
maybe next time we will
go out in the pouring rain.

Nellie the Dragon

Nellie the dragon
Was not very well
Because her fire
It had gone out,
She went to see
The master dragon
To find how this
Came about.
She was told
The reason it was
Because she had
A dragon flu,
And then he told
Her what to do.
He told her to
Go home and rest,
Then she will be
Back to her best.

North Pole Rush

Christmas is coming
and the fairies and elves,
are making toys
to put onto shelves.
The snow outside
is falling fast,
they must work
like every day's the last.
Till they're finished and
they can say,
let's all load them
on the sleigh.
The reindeers are ready
Santa says "Ho ho ho",
cos round the world
he's ready to go.
And every child
on Christmas Day,
will get their gifts
hip hip hooray.

Nursery Madness

Hey diddle diddle,
the cats got a riddle
why did the cow
go to the moon,
to find the dog,
who got lost
in the fog.
While he was
playing a tune.

Nursery Mayhem

Jack n jill
Went down the hill
For they were
Having a meet,
It was with their friends
Down a little street.
Little boy blue
And Margery daw,
They all went
To the store.
Afterwards went
Out for tea,
And finally got
Home by three.

Nursery Party

Polly put the kettle on
cos she was
making tea,
she was having
a visit from
Little Jack Horner
and Jack Sprat
made three.
Little Jack Horner
brought round his pie,
he thought he would
share it he said
with a sigh.
Jack Sprat brought
all his lean meat,
and Polly had a cake
for a special treat.
A good time was
had by all,
who said let's do it
again next fall.

Ode to Santa

I will sing an
Ode to Santa
He's there every year,
coming in on
his sleigh to
bring some
Christmas cheer.
He is there to bring joy,
for each girl and
every boy.
So, sing with me
and make it loud,
for of Santa
we are proud.

Party Time

Pat-a-cake pat-a-cake
baker's man,
we need cakes as
fast as you can.
For today we are
going to have a party.
We will be just
hale and hearty.

Little Boy Blue is coming
and also Little Bo Peep,
have to do it early before
she goes to sleep.

Humpty Dumpty is
off the wall,
cos no one gave
him a call.
So, my friends all
you have to do,
Is get to my party
today at half past two.

Princesses Ball

Once upon a time
twas in fairyland,
there was a special ball
it was so very grand.
Where all the lovely
Princesses went out
for the night,
with their lovely
dresses on
oh, they did look
a sight.
They danced
and danced and
had fairy cakes
and fairy drink
then a charming
Prince came by
and gave them
all a wink.
Then fairy godmother came
and said
it's time you
Princesses all
went home
and I'll tuck
you all in bed.

Purple Space

This is a special place
that is a purple space
this is a waiting room
for witches waiting
for a broom.
Although this does
sound tragic,
fairies wait here
for their magic.
And as a must,
they also get
some fairy dust.
So, if you go
to Fairyland
And looking
for a prop
so go around
to purple space
it is the ideal shop.

The Queen of Fairyland

I'm the queen
of fairyland
sitting here
oh so grand.
I can sit for hours,
looking at all
the lovely flowers.
And keeping an
eye on Fairyland,
make sure life is
always grand.
I love to watch
the butterflies
the birds and
all the bees
with nature
at its very best
to me it
doth please.
And as the day
comes to the end
I get filled with
sorrow,
but there is always
another day
I'll look forward
to tomorrow.

Red Riding Hood

One day Red Riding Hood
went to see
her Grandmama,
she had to
walk through the forest
as she didn't
have a car.
People said Grandma
had turned into a beast,
but that was a typing error
she was sitting for a feast.

Snow White Night

Snow White went
out one night
cos she had a date,
it was with the
Seven Dwarves
at twenty-five past eight.
Cos she was so greedy
just one wouldn't do,
so they all went
to have some dinner
and a booga loo.
When it came
to midnight
they all went home
to rest,
and Snow White said
to the seven dwarves
tonight it was the best

Three Little Pigs

Once upon a time
in days of old,
there were
three pigs
very cold.
So, they built a
house of straw,
till the Big Bad Wolf
came to the door.
So, they got out
it was
half past six,
they did build
a house of sticks.
But then just as before,
that bad old wolf
knocked at the door.
Well, they got out
said no more tricks
we're having a house
made of bricks.
So, once they paid
the grafter
they lived happily
ever after.

Toyland

Toyland is a place
where teddy bears walk,
and dolls like to sit
down and have a talk.
Where there's a castle
called Lego Fort,
and you can grow
even if you're short.
Where train sets
come to life and
take you for a ride,
for its very spacious
if you go inside.
And when you have
had your Toyland tour,
maybe next year you
can come back
for more.

Unicorn

I am the astra
the unicorn and
I have got lost,
went to find
a rainbow but
didn't realise
the cost.
Went thru the fairy kingdom
but didn't know,
that a rainbow came
where the blueberries grow.
Then someone found me
just past the mountain,
said you will find
the rainbow
just past the magic fountain.

Vanitia a Fairy Tale

Vanitia was a fairy
she was so very vain,
all the fairies say
there's Vanitia
looking in the
mirror again.
One day Vanitia's mother,
she just had enough
she got rid of the mirror
she found it
oh, so tough.
Then Vanitia's friends
asked her out to play,
and she realised that
now the mirrors gone
she was having fun
every single day.

The Wedding

It was a big day
in Fairyland everyone
was there,
wanted to let you know
so, we can happiness share.
For there was to
be a wedding and
a beautiful cake,
for an ideal couple
there won't be
no mistake.
It's Thumbelina
and Tom Thumb
Who are walking down
the aisle,
all the elves have arrived
with their little smile.
So, put your hands together
and shout a big hooray,
we must celebrate on
their special day.

X is the Spot.

X marks the spot
where the fairies go
it is near the glen,
they always know
where to find it
it's written with
a fairy pen.
It's the only way
that they can go
you can hear their chatter,
when their little feet go
pitter pitter patter.
Then you will understand
they will be back
safe in Fairyland.

Yellow Land

I have just
found a land
it is as yellow
as can be,
On the beach
There's yellow sand
near a yellow tree.
It's a land of magic
with a lovely
yellow cloud,
it looks so pretty
I want to
shout out loud.
And if you want
a special treat,
there's always lots
of yellow things to eat.
Lemons, bananas and
mallows too,
and when the
yellow sun comes out
it has a tint of blue.
So, if you want a place
that is so unique,
come along with me
cos I'm going
there next week.

Zoo for Magical Animals

There is a magic land,
where everything is
oh so grand.
And if you go
through the magic wood,
this I really think
you should.
There lies a magic zoo,
such wonderful animals
there and a snowy owl
that goes to whit to woo.
There's dragons and unicorns
and Pegasus you see,
he is a winged horse you
can see them all for free.
There's also a magic cat
that can also fly,
and don't forget
the magic brook
when you come on by.
Cos there you will see,
the mermaids swimming
all with lots of glee.
So, when you come to
this magic land you
must all enjoy,
this wonderful magic zoo
for every girl and every boy.

About the Author

My name is Ruth Doyle.

I come from London originally and now I live in Essex with my sons.
I come from a family that have been given the gift of writing poetry. My sisters are very good at writing poetry but I thought I would go a step further and decided it would be nice if I could share it.
The nearest I have come to publishing previously was entering competitions, but that was about 30 years ago.

I hope these poems are enjoyed by all.

Printed in Great Britain
by Amazon

83459970R00037